NEW ENGLAND

NEW ENGLAND

Upper reaches of the Connecticut River, longest waterway in New England (nearly 400 miles) as it approaches Pittsburg, New Hampshire. It flows south forming the boundary between New Hampshire and Vermont, through Massachusetts and Connecticut, where it empties into Long Island Sound. In background, weather-worn bridge appears structurally sound in this moisture-laden region.

PHOTOGRAPHY BY CLYDE H. SMITH

TEXT BY ANN GLICKMAN

International Standard Book Number 0-912856-17-3
Library of Congress Catalog Number 74-33866
Copyright© 1975 by Publisher • Charles H. Belding
Graphic Arts Center Publishing Co.
2000 N.W. Wilson • Portland, Oregon 97209 • 503/224-7777
Designer • Robert Reynolds
Text • Ann Glickman
Printer • Graphic Arts Center
Bindery • Lincoln & Allen
Paper manufactured by S. D. Warren Paper Co., Boston, Mass.
Printed in the United States of America

Closeup of oak leaves
at sunset in western
Connecticut.

Dense grove of white birch in autumn; southern Vermont. Left: Farm near Cambridge, Vermont. In background is 4,393 foot Mt. Mansfield.

Elm trees in swamp during January thaw, near Shelburne, Vermont.

Canada goose at Audubon
Refuge, near Sharon,
Connecticut. Right: Yellow
birch robed in autumn
foliage near Huntington,
Vermont. In the distance
Camel's Hump. Pages 12-13,
A chilling winter morning
near Rutland, Vermont.

Winter skiing offers fun and
excitement on summit ridge
of Mt. Mansfield, Vermont.
Robert Webb, age 14,
is on his way down.

NEW ENGLAND

If we had no winter, the spring would not be pleasant:
If we did not sometimes taste of adversity, prosperity
would not be so welcome.

ANNE BRADSTREET (1612-1672)

New England has the same highways, skyscrapers, supermarkets, and fast food chains found in other regions of the United States, but the features one remembers are not these. The images that stay in one's mind are white churches set on green commons; stone walls along the sides of roads or running to nowhere through the woods; covered bridges on forgotten routes; clusters of farm buildings attached to one another; the rocky coast of Maine; the Berkshire Hills ablaze with autumn foliage. New England comprises a particular union of natural resources and human landmarks found in no other part of America.

The region is made up of six separate states: Maine, New Hampshire, Vermont, Massachusetts, Rhode Island, and Connecticut. But to the traveller these political divisions are relatively unimportant. Much more striking is the impression that the region is a single entity. Partly this is because the six states have a common history. Equally important is the fact that they are united by climate, geography, and geology.

New England is bordered to the east and the south by ocean. Its rugged coastline forms 6,000 miles of inlets, coves, and bays from Calais, Maine, in the north to Greenwich, Connecticut, in the south. To the west it is divided from New York by Lake Champlain and the Adirondack Mountains. Canada forms a national boundary to the north. Historically, New England has been apart from other parts of the country due to its geography.

The whole region was once covered with glaciers that left beds of broken granite in their wake. Most of Connecticut and western Massachusetts are part of a huge peneplain in which valleys have been carved; thus, the land is not a flat plain but two groups of gently rolling hills: the Litchfield Hills in Connecticut and the Berkshire Hills in Massachusetts. Further north, in the center of Vermont, the plain rises to form the Green Mountains. These run all the way to the Canadian border. The highest peak in Vermont is Mount Mansfield (4,394 feet) at Stowe. None

of these mountains are high by western standards, for geologically they are very old and have been worn down into rounded hills. In New Hampshire are found the White Mountains, much younger and therefore more dramatic. The elevation of these peaks is not high—Mount Washington is only 6,288 feet above sea level—but they rise steeply from the valleys at their feet. Between the Green and White Mountains runs the Connecticut River. As it travels south through Massachusetts and into Connecticut it forms a wide valley that has attracted farmers since the Puritans first arrived in Massachusetts. Other major rivers include the Merrimack, which runs from New Hampshire into Massachusetts, where it empties into the Atlantic at Newburyport, and the Housatonic, which runs down the western part of Connecticut to Long Island Sound.

Living off the land has always been a terrible struggle in New England, because the topsoil is poor and the climate extreme. Seasons vary dramatically, from freezing, penetrating cold in the winter to debilitating heat in the summer. The growing season is short and unpredictable, and farmers must use their instinct and experience to figure out exactly the right time to plant and to harvest. If frost comes after planting or before harvesting, produce may be destroyed. In Maine the year has been described as "nine months of winter and three months of damn poor sleddin'."

But New England is also a beautiful place, as these photographs express more eloquently than words. Perhaps it is the combination of beauty and challenge that has drawn people here for more than three hundred years, beginning with the Pilgrims. What have people found in New England? And how have they helped to shape its character and features?

PLYMOUTH PLANTATION

After long beating at sea they fell with that land which is called Cape Cod. Being thus arrived in a good harbor, and brought safe to land, they fell upon their knees and blessed the God of Heaven who had brought them over the vast and furious ocean, and delivered them from all [its] perils and miseries, to set their feet on the firm and stable earth. . . .

Being thus passed the vast ocean . . . they had now no friends to welcome them nor inns to entertain or refresh their weather-beaten bodies; no houses or much less towns to repair to, to seek for succor. And for the season it was winter, and they that know the winters of that country know them to be sharp and violent, and subject to cruel and fierce storms, dangerous to travel in, much more to search an unknown coast. Besides what could they see but a hideous and desolate wilderness, full of wild beasts and wild men, and what multitudes of them they knew not. [The] whole country, full of woods and thickets, had a wild and savage hue. If they looked behind them, there was the sea which they had passed and was now as a main bar and gulf to separate them from all civil parts of the world. What could now sustain them but the spirit of God and His grace?

WILLIAM BRADFORD (1590-1657)

New England's past began, as every school child knows, at Plymouth. Actually it began much earlier, with Indians who lived here for centuries, with explorers seeking a northern route to the fabled East, with fishermen who found riches in the sea in the form of cod. The reports of these early European visitors—that the land was green and bountiful (they neglected to mention the harsh winters), that the Indians were peaceful and willing to trade—interested people in England like Sir John Popham and Sir Ferdinando Gorges. In 1607, the same year that settlers arrived in Jamestown, Virginia, a group of people backed by Popham and Gorges arrived in Atkins Bay, Maine, led by Sir John's brother Gilbert. The Indians weren't helpful, the group wasn't well organized, and the winter was severe. In spring, when Gilbert was called back to England, the others abandoned the settlement.

What finally did bring settlers to New England were the same forces that had been at work throughout Europe and for a century in England had been building stronger and stronger demands for civil and religious liberty. The most radical English dissenters wanted to flee from the Church of England altogether. Called Separatists, they were so harassed by Crown and Church that many left for Leyden, Holland, where they were free to practice religion in their own way. Commercial Leyden didn't suit them, however, and they began to think of the New World.

In 1620, a group of separatists sailed to America with several English families and indentured servants who were not members of their church. They were backed by a group of English investors who called themselves "Merchant Adventurers." They had a patent from the London Company giving them a site on the Hudson River, but they never got there. Whether storms and dangerous reefs caused them to turn north when they reached Cape Cod, or whether the Separatists thought they would be free of Anglican authority outside of Virginia, is unclear. The passengers argued heatedly about what to do, but their leaders chose to sail to present-day Provincetown near the tip of Cape Cod. From there a search party went out and found the site that became their home one month later: an abandoned Indian village which they named "Plimoth Plantation."

The Pilgrims arrived at Cape Cod in November, 1620, after a long and rough crossing. Many people were sick. During the voyage they had protected themselves against scurvy by drinking beer, but that was now in short supply. As winter drew on, many people died. The handful of men and women who remained healthy looked after those who were ill. They might all have died, but the Indians of that region befriended them.

Europeans were not unknown to the New England Indians because they had been dealing with fishermen, trappers, and hunters for some years. Feelings about the Europeans varied. Some Indians saw them as enemies encroaching on their lands, while others viewed them as potential allies and friends. The Pilgrims were lucky. After a few first wary encounters with the Indians, they established good relations with them. Their greatest political ally was the chief of the Wampanoag Indian tribe, Massasoit (1580-1661), who accepted them and convinced other tribes to trade with them. He remained a faithful friend until death, forty years later.

A second great friend, although he lived only two years after their arrival, was Squanto. Squanto had been captured some years earlier and taken to England where he learned to speak English. On a trip back to America he escaped and eventually made his way back to his village, only to find that his tribe had been wiped out by pestilence. Squanto came to live with the Pilgrims. He showed them how and when to plant corn (their

18

English seeds and wheat fared poorly), and advised them that "except they got fish and set with [the corn] in these old grounds it would come to nothing." William Bradford, governor of Plymouth, described Squanto "as a special instrument sent by God for their good beyond their expectation."

The colony survived, though half its number died that first year. It engaged in trade as soon as possible, obtaining beaver pelts from the Indians to send to England with lumber, dried fish, sassafras, tar, and pitch. Within a few years the colony had bought out its backers and become self-supporting. It continued as an independent colony until 1691, when William and Mary made it part of Massachusetts Bay Colony.

Today Plymouth Plantation attracts visitors from everywhere.

THE PURITAN EXPERIMENT

We shall be as a city upon a hill, the eyes of all people are upon us; so that if we shall deal falsely with our God in this work we have undertaken and so cause Him to withdraw His present aid, we shall be made a story and a by-word through the world.

JOHN WINTHROP (1588-1649)

John Winthrop was a landowner with a background in law and several years experience settling disputes between landowners and the king. He was a dedicated Puritan who believed in working through existing institutions such as Parliament to bring about changes that he felt were morally necessary, particularly within the Church of England. In 1629, when Charles I dismissed Parliament, clearly intending to call it into session no more, the Puritans lost an important forum. Some began to talk of going to New England. A small group of Puritans had already started a small town on Massachusetts Bay, which they called Salem (from "Shalom," the Hebrew word meaning peace). As a respected leader, Winthrop knew that if he chose to go hundreds of Puritans would join him. Could he accept responsibility for leading them on such a dangerous undertaking? If he stayed, he would be supporting a government he believed was evil. If he left, he would be accused of running away from battle. Winthrop struggled with this dilemma and finally came to believe that God intended him to establish a Puritan colony in America.

From King Charles the Puritans obtained a charter to set up a trading company with rights extending from the Charles River north to the Merrimack River and running east to west "from sea to sea." The charter stipulated that a governing council be set up, but neglected to say that the council must meet in London. Winthrop convinced others in his group that if they took the charter with them the council could legitimately meet in Massachusetts. They could establish a self-ruling colony instead of a trading company with London overseers. Winthrop's daring proposition was accepted. When he and several hundred followers arrived in Salem, they had the charter with them. The new group chose to settle south of Salem at the mouth of the Charles River, the site of present-day Boston.

The Puritans believed government was based on a covenant between God and His people, and that a good government was one that enforced God's laws as stated in the Bible. They found many analogies between themselves and the ancient Israelites whom Moses led out of Egypt to the promised land. Like the Israelites, they saw themselves building a Zion in the wilderness, "a city upon a hill."

One of the colony's first laws was that no one could settle there until his or her orthodoxy was approved by the governing council of magistrates. In order to build a society that would be a model for the rest of the world, every member of that society had to be a "visible saint." Historian Daniel Boorstin says, "The energies which their English contemporaries gave to sharpening the distinctions between 'compulsive' and 'restrictive' powers in religion . . . and to a host of other questions . . . the American Puritans were giving to marking off the boundaries of their new towns, to enforcing their criminal laws, and to fighting the Indian menace. . . . Had they spent as much of their energy in debating with each other as did their English counterparts, they might have lacked the single-mindedness needed to overcome the dark, unpredictable perils of a wilderness."

The Puritans were eminently successful in settling the wilderness. By 1640, ten years after Winthrop's arrival, there were 16,000 English settlers in Massachusetts.

The most important figure in any Puritan community was the minister, and the most important community event the Sabbath-day service when everyone collected to hear his sermon. The minister had tremendous power over people's minds, but his power was not absolute. Unlike the Catholic and Anglican bishops and priests, Puritan ministers were not chosen by the heads of the church but by members of the individual congregations. One of the Puritans' chief points of dissent with the Church of England was its hierarchical structure. They believed that people who had revealed their religious worth through faith and good works were capable of running their own congregations. The congregation could both choose and unseat its minister. A prominent Puritan minister, John Cotton, said: "It is most wholesome for Magistrates and Officers in Church and Commonwealth never to affect more liberty and authority than will do them good, and the People good. . . . There is a strain in a man's heart that will sometime or other run out to excess, unless the Lord restrain it, but it is not good to venture it: It is necessary therefore that all power that is on earth be limited." The belief that leaders are responsible to the people they serve is a basic tenet of American government. While Winthrop's colony was by no means a democracy, the seeds of participatory government and accountability were there.

Anglican sermons were filled with visual imagery: color, metaphor, decoration. To the Puritans the unadorned word was paramount. They looked for hard, literal truths in their sermons. The sermon was the chief means for influencing people's behavior and thinking. Therefore, it was important that people be literate, that they be able to read the scriptures themselves and be able to understand the sermons and take notes. The Puritans were interested in preparing youth for serving Church and state, in keeping would-be idlers off the streets, and in thwarting "that old deluder, Satan," by enabling children to read the scriptures. All communities of fifty families or more were required to provide schools—an extraordinary concept in an age of general illiteracy. While the schools were not free, they were available, and some towns did levy taxes to help pay for them. The Massachusetts law was later adopted by Connecticut and the northern colonies. At the time of the Revolution, Rhode Island was the only New England colony that did not require schools.

One reason the Puritans placed such a high value on education is that they themselves were well educated. In the 1630s, Massachusetts probably had more university graduates than any other area of its size in the world. One of the first needs the magistrates faced was the establishment of a university, primarily for the training of ministers but also for the maintenance of a high level of culture within the society. The book *New England's First Fruits*, published in 1643, includes this passage:

After God had carried us safe to New England, and we had built our houses, provided necessaries for our livelihood, reared convenient places for God's worship, and settled the Civil Government: One of the next things we longed for, and looked after was to advance Learning, *and perpetuate it to Posterity; dreading to leave an illiterate Ministery to the Churches, when our present Ministers shall lie in the Dust. And as we were thinking and consulting how to effect this great Work, it pleased God to stir up the heart of one Mr.* Harvard, *a godly Gentlemen and a lover of Learning, there living amongst us, to give the one half of his Estate, toward the erecting of a college, and all his Library. After him another gave 300 [pounds]. Others after them cast in more, and the public hand of the State added the rest: the College was, by common consent, appointed to be at Cambridge, a place very pleasant and accommodate, and is called (according to the name of the first founder)* Harvard College.

Throughout its history New England has been a leader in providing education. The general level of literacy declined during the 1700s, but in the 1800s the movement for public school reform began in New England. Today New England's colleges and universities provide training for many of the country's top leaders in business, medicine, the sciences, law, and other professions.

The Puritans also laid the foundation for New England town government. There were many reasons why early settlers who started new communities in the wilderness chose to do so in groups. Fear of Indians, of wild animals, of isolation and ignorance about how to survive in the woods were powerful forces that kept people together. Religion was another strong influence. No family could risk traveling through the dense and terrifying woods to come to meeting on the Sabbath, and in winter travel was almost impossible before roads were built.

Finally, living in groups was more congenial, and even people who spent their long winter evenings reading the Bible or doing constructive work craved social activity. For all these reasons early settlements were generally begun by groups of relatives and close friends. From the colonial government in Boston they could receive authority to establish a town government. This gave them the power to raise and spend money. The governments they formed were essentially cooperative in nature. Decisions about group welfare were made at a town meeting attended by every adult member of the church. Boston was as far away as London, in terms of how much influence it exerted on towns. The result was that people became used to making decisions that affected their local affairs.

Not everyone found Winthrop's colony to his or her liking. Thomas Hooker, a minister in Cambridge, objected to the law that a person had to be a church member in order to have a voice in civil affairs. Everyone who settled in Massachusetts had to have his or her orthodoxy approved by the magistrates. But this did not mean that everyone automatically became a church member. The governing magistrates decided who belonged to the church and who didn't, which gave them the power to choose their constituency. When Hooker realized that there was no possibility of changing this policy, he and members of his congregation obtained permission to start a settlement outside of Massachusetts, in what is now Hartford, Connecticut. There, with residents of Windsor and Wethersfield, a new colony was set up in 1639 and named Connecticut. Unlike Massachusetts, which lost its charter in 1692, Connecticut remained independent throughout the colonial era.

Roger Williams, a resident of Salem, came into direct conflict with the magistrates over the question of civil and religious power. He believed the state would corrupt the church unless the two areas of power were kept separate. Williams came to be seen as dangerous to the very existence of the colony and was banished. With a few followers he set out for what is now Providence, Rhode Island, where he established a colony in 1636 that also remained independent until the Revolution.

Anne Hutchinson was another critic who became dangerous in the eyes of the magistrates. A highly educated Englishwoman, Anne Hutchinson came from a family that included the poet John Dryden. She became a supporter of Winthrop in England, and followed him to Massachusetts with her husband and fifteen children. A dedicated member of the church, she was disturbed that the one area of religious life from which women were excluded was discussion of church doctrine. To correct this situation she began inviting ministers to her home to discuss doctrine with groups of women. The conversation was probing, the minds unwilling to be sedated. Ministers and magistrates grew alarmed. When Anne Hutchinson began calling for a reform of church doctrine she too was banished. With her family and several friends, she went to Rhode Island. Members of the Hutchinson group started settlements at Portsmouth in 1638 and Newport in 1639. After her husband died she and her children moved to New York. A few years later they perished during an Indian attack.

There were even Puritans who found Winthrop's government too lax. Two of the original founders, Theophilus Eaton and John Davenport, left to found a colony at New Haven in 1637 that would adhere more closely to Mosaic law. In Massachusetts Mosaic law had been judged too severe. Diametrically opposed in their convictions to the Connecticut settlers, New Haven's citizens were dismayed when Charles II gave Connecticut jurisdiction over them in 1662.

The Puritan political experiment ended in 1692, when England began appointing royal governors, who were Anglicans, to oversee the colony's affairs. But the Puritan religion, the foundation of the Congregational Church, continued to be the dominant religion, and the patterns of political, social, and moral behavior begun during the Puritan era continued to shape the character of New England people. There were other strains besides straight-and-narrow religious zeal, however. These early settlers were earthy, blunt, pragmatic. While working to build a society for God they enjoyed the fruits of their labor. By the time of the Revolution they had evolved into a society of spirited Yankees.

CONFRONTING THE WILDERNESS
It will be easily believed that the labors . . . must be attended by fatigue and hardships sufficient to discourage any man who can

live tolerably on his native soil. But the principal sufferings of these planters . . . spring from quite other sources. The want of neighbors to assist them, the want of convenient implements, and universally the want of those means without which the necessary business of life cannot be carried on even comfortably is among their greatest difficulties . . .

The common troubles of life scarcely awaken in them the slightest emotion. The coarsest food is pleasant, and the hardest bed refreshing. Cold and heat, snow and rain, labor and fatigue are regarded by them as trifles.

Every case of distress is easily realized by all, because all have been sufferers. This vivid sympathy spreads cheerfulness and resolution where a traveler would look for little else besides discouragement and gloom.

TIMOTHY DWIGHT (1752-1817)

Timothy Dwight, who was at one time president of Yale College, was referring to the back woods settlers he met while traveling through the White Mountains in 1797. By this time, Indian attacks were only a memory: a story handed down from generation to generation, the fabric of children's fantasy. People did not always strike out for the wilderness in groups anymore; sometimes a man might live alone for months at a time, hacking away at the hated trees to make a spot where corn and beans would grow and a house for his family would be built. Whether they set out alone or with their families, those who cleared the wilderness faced common hardships and looked for similar rewards. For once a clearing was made and a farm built, the family could look forward to years of increasing comfort and prosperity. In England they had lived as tenants on some other family's manor; here they owned their own land and could start a farm that would be carried on by their children and their children's children.

For one hundred and fifty years settlement followed the rivers, and these only as far as they were navigable. Travel through the woods was almost impossible. There were no roads, and what animal paths did exist were narrow, covered with fallen trees, and dangerously perched on the edges of cliffs. Once farms were built, families needed the river to transport produce to seacoast markets and to carry back supplies such as salt, tea, and cooking pots.

It is hard to imagine carving a farm out of the wilderness with a few hand tools and little know-how but people did it. Colonial historian Louis Wright says, "Tools and implements essential to a modern expedition were utterly unknown to seventeenth-century colonists. They had their bare hands, a few axes, hand-saws, adzes, wedges, mauls, picks, shovels, and hoes. With these implements they had to fell trees, shape timbers for their houses, rive clapboards and shingles, and erect their buildings."

At first people lived in crude shelters of mud and sticks or in caves dug out of the sides of hills. They learned to hunt deer, pigeons, and wild turkeys, to snare rabbits and squirrels, to catch fish. Many adopted the Indian garb, deerskin, which afforded better protection than wool from thorns and branches. Faced with removing a forest tree by tree, they cut and chopped endlessly, or used the Indians' labor-saving method of girdling trees: stripping a thin circle of bark from the base of the tree, cutting off its food supply. In time the tree would die and fall. In this way small patches of land were cleared slowly, and corn, wheat, beans, and pumpkins planted among the stumps and rocks. It was many generations before fields were fully cleared. Timothy Dwight complained of "the uncouth and disgusting aspect of fields left with many dry trees standing, and others blown down and lying in every direction." The practice of girdling trees eventually fell into disuse. The preferred method became chopping down trees, making piles of wood, and burning them. This created a residue of ashes which could be left to fertilize the soil or packed up and sold: ash was an important ingredient of soap and commanded a good price.

Eventually a permanent house was built, typically modeled after the dwellings the settlers had known in England: frame houses with steeply pitched roofs. The simpler log cabin, which provided a first home for later settlers, was not known to these Englishmen; it was brought here by the Germans and the Swedes. The plainest house was a single room with a chimney at one end and a dirt floor. For decoration, the wife or daughter might trace designs in the dirt with a stick. A sleeping loft, the warmest part of the house, might be built under the peaked roof and reached by a ladder or narrow stairway. In time a second room might be added on the other side of the chimney.

Larger houses followed this same pattern, but some had rooms on three sides of the chimney, a second story, and even a small attic. The largest ground floor room was the kitchen/living room. In the seventeenth century the second floor might overhang the first by a foot or two, a custom in England; gradually this custom disappeared. Windows were covered with oilskin or oiled paper, wooden shutters, or precious panes of glass imported from England. Sometimes a small room was added at one end. The rafters leaned against the existing wall, so the room was called a leanto. The rafters extended the roof slope nearly to the ground on one side. Later generations referred to this type of house as a "salt box," because it resembled the containers salt used to come in; such houses are still a common feature of the New England landscape. The shape was not only pleasing but functional, for the longer roof slope, usually facing north, broke the winter wind.

Houses were not insulated for many years. Families could expect to wake up in winter and find snow on their quilts and ice in their wash basins. Eventually people learned to stuff corn cobs or newspapers into walls to keep out the cold.

Each room was apt to be filled with an incongruous clutter of objects, for it had to serve many purposes: kitchen, tool workshop, bedroom, nursery, spinning and weaving room. Furniture was simple and functional. A seventeenth-century home featured a trestle table and benches, chests for storage, beds, one of which might stand on end against the kitchen wall, concealed by a door or curtain and perhaps a chair or two. Up to the nineteenth century chairs were light because they were moved often, either being pulled closer to the fire for warmth or next to the window for light.

The fireplace was the most important feature of the house, serving as both furnace and stove. It was outfitted with a crane and hooks for hanging kettles and pots. But most cooking was done directly on the hearth: a pile of coals would be made there, over which a "spider", a large trivet, was set. Herbs, used both for flavoring and medicine, hung from the rafters in front of the fireplace to dry.

In the seventeenth century, food was eaten out of large wooden bowls called trenchers, which were usually shared by two or more family members. Governor Winthrop had the distinction of owning a fork; he may have been the only colonist to have one for many years. Utensils, when they were used at all for eating, were spoons. Most people managed with their hands and napkins the size of small tablecloths.

At least as important as the house were storage buildings and animal shelters. Early silos for storing corn were actually pits lined with stones and ashes and covered with husks. Cellars dug into the sides of hills provided storage for meats and vegetables. In order for a barn to be built, or even a frame house, a family needed neighbors. They could make the timbers, boards, and shingles themselves, but they couldn't raise the frame without the help of many hands. The frame was built in the following way: Logs hewn into square timbers with a broad axe were notched to receive the ends of crossbeams. Beams were hammered into place with a wooden mallet weighing fifty pounds. Wooden pegs anchored the pieces together. When the frame for each side had been constructed in this way, neighbors were called in to help. Each man brought his pike pin, a long pole with a sharp blade on the end, with which he would help push a frame piece from the ground into the air. It would be held in place with pikes and ropes until the next side was raised and joined to it. In this manner men and boys could raise a frame in a twenty-four hour period, after which they celebrated with food and entertainment. The siding, rafters, and shingles came later, all of them cut by axe.

The barn was used for storing grain and hay and sheltering horses, pigs, and sheep. (Early settlers brought livestock with them from England.) Other buildings that the family might add in time were tool sheds, poultry house, sheep shed, and spring house. The family would also build its own saw pit, grist mill, and blacksmith shed, unless a town with these facilities was nearby.

When covered bridges began to appear early in the nineteenth century, they were constructed in a fashion similar to frame houses and barns, except that first the floor supports had to be "thrown" across the stream. The reason for covering bridges was to protect them from weather and lengthen their life. The difficulty they presented is that in winter people traveled by pungs and sleighs which had runners instead of wheels. Snow had to be shoveled onto the bridge before they could pass over.

The fences most often associated with New England are stone walls, but these were not the earliest fences. Sometimes a barrier was made by shoveling dirt into a ridge and covering it with brush. A tangle of tree roots was another type of fence. Some people also made split rail fences. Mortarless stone fences developed when people had more time for removing rocks and piling them up along the side of fields. Those that still stand today were carefully and ingeniously constructed. They begin three feet below ground and have a base wider than the top to provide anchorage against frost heaves.

Some time in the 1700s, probably in New Hampshire, the custom arose of attaching all farm buildings to the main house so that the family would not have to go outdoors in winter to feed their animals and repair their farm equipment. In some towns ordinances were passed prohibiting this practice and requiring that barns be placed several feet away from the house. The reason was that barns, with their store of drying hay and grain, were a terrible fire hazard. The custom persisted however, and eventually the restrictions were dropped. Today attached farm buildings can be seen throughout New England, particularly in Maine, New Hampshire, and Vermont.

It is difficult to imagine the loneliness and isolation experienced by the first back woods settlers. One young wife felt a tremendous relief when her husband began chopping down trees and a mountain sprang into view; that mountain was her close companion for the rest of her life. Two women who were neighbors in the White Mountains rarely saw each other because their homes were separated by an impassable gully. To reach one another's home by the blazed path around the gully took the good part of a day. But each woman listened each day for thumping, a sign that her neighbor was pounding grain by hand. Eventually the women contrived a code and learned to send greetings and news by thumping. So well did they understand each other that a few hours after one gave birth to twins the other arrived to congratulate her.

LIVING IN TOWNS

The oldest towns appeared along the coast, in Connecticut, Rhode Island, and Massachusetts, with a handful of settlements located in New Hampshire and Maine. For as long as possible people chose natural clearings. Vermont, most of New Hampshire, and Maine did not begin to settle thickly until well into the eighteenth century. Vermont in earlier years was a hunting and battle ground for the Algonquin tribes of upper New York, much too dangerous a place for farmsteaders. As the eighteenth century unfolded, New Hampshire attracted an increasing number of settlers who stayed near the coast or settled west of the White Mountains along the Connecticut River; northern communities were extremely isolated because of the mountains. In Maine, English settlement followed the coves and harbors along its coast, most of the interior being controlled by the French. After the last French and Indian war ended in English victory in 1763, France gave up all claim to northern New England and English settlement began in earnest. Vermont, whose permanent population was 300 in 1760, had a quarter of a million people by 1810. When Maine gained entrance to the Union in 1820, its population was 300,000.

One of the differences between New England and other parts of the country is that farms did not lie outside of town but were part of the town itself. Thus, the geographical size of a town tended to be large, even if its population was not. Once an area had attracted about thirty families, the settlers could take steps to establish a town. The first requirement was that they build a meeting house and invite a minister. His living was guaranteed by the town and usually included a house, a farm, and such services as a steady supply of firewood. Then the residents could petition the colonial government for town status, which enabled them to build and maintain roads and a school and provide for such needs as the care of the poor. The names they selected for their towns often recalled older civilizations—Goshen, Canaan, Jericho—or towns in England—Chelsea, Dover, Essex, New London, Southampton, or exotic-sounding parts of Europe—Berlin, Paris, Norway.

The pattern on which the earliest towns was based came from England. In feudal days, English villages grew up on hills because high ground was easier to defend. New Englanders also located their early towns on hills, partly as protection from Indian attack but also because the ground was easier to clear and till. In the earliest towns the center contained a large grazing area for sheep and other livestock, surrounded by the meeting house and homes. Once Indians were no longer a threat, families preferred to move out onto their land; communal ownership broke down, but the practice of having a town common, the site of the meeting house, prevailed. Eventually a town might spread over a huge area and include several villages, clusters of ten or fifteen families living near each other, but the center village was always the site of the meeting house.

The meeting house was the hub of the town's religious, civil, and social life. Like the homes, it was a clapboard structure. The earliest meeting houses were built with the long side facing the common and the door in the center. In the nineteenth century, the shorter, gabled end of the building faced front. Many meeting houses had a tower, sometimes built years after the original structure, which contained a bell and a clock. Early towers jutted out from the front of the building. Eventually the towers receded into the main structure, becoming thin, graceful spires tapering off to a fine point.

Inside the meeting house the focal center was not an altar but the pulpit, a wooden cage raised above the floor of the building and reached by a flight of steps. At first the congregation sat on benches. Later, each family paid for its own pew, a square, wooden pen with seats on three sides. The family's standing in the community was clearly shown by the location of its pew, the most prominent citizens being closest to the pulpit. When hymns, which were never heard in early Puritan meetings, became part of the Sabbath services in the eighteenth century, meeting houses included a gallery above the ground floor for the choir. The meeting house was not heated, and the temperature in winter was often close to freezing. Women were allowed to bring foot stoves, but men and boys had to suffer in manly fashion. Since services took up most of the Sabbath Day, their discomfort must have been intense. In the languid heat of summer it was easy to fall asleep, particularly if the minister was harping on a theme that had long ago grown tiresome. To com-

bat this people brought sprigs of fennel or dill to sniff. One man devised an elaborate warning system: Being bald, he let the hair on the sides of his face grow long, and he tied the side locks together on top of his head with a string. Whenever his head nodded, the ends of the string dropped onto his eyelids and woke him up.

Adjoining the meeting house was the burying ground and the town school was nearby. Most eighteenth-century towns also had a tavern near the common, where stagecoach travelers and families coming in to meeting could stop for meals. One coach stop in Whitman, Massachusetts, called the Toll House, became famous for its cookies. Taverns were informal and popular meeting houses, drawing people in for hot toddies, gossip, and relaxation.

In late eighteenth-century towns, besides farmers, a minister, and a doctor there were people who spent at least part of their time in trade and craft activities. If a town had water power, it might host a sawmill, where people brought their logs to be cut into fireplace lengths or timber; and a grist mill, where corn, rye, and wheat were ground into flour. Often these mills supplied the needs of more than one town, and their owners became prosperous. Most towns also had a blacksmith shop, which made iron tools, and one or more stores which sold cooking pots and porcelain, buttons, combs, spices, tea, salt, and possibly hard cider and rum. In *Quabbin: The Story of a Small Town*, Francis Underwood describes the store he remembered most vividly in his childhood, around the 1820s:

The principal store of the town is remembered chiefly by its permanent odor, in which there were suggestions of dried codfish, pickled mackerel, spices, snuff, plug tobacco, molasses, and new rum, reinforced in cold weather by the evaporation of tobacco juice upon a hot stove, and the occasional whiff of a pipe. The storekeeper was quiet and shrewd, and knew the cumulative power of compound interest. A farmer who had fallen behind-hand could get a continuance of supplies, including the indispensable jug, by giving a mortgage upon his land, a backward step which was seldom retrieved, so that in the course of years the storekeeper's roofs might have been measured in acres. He was not in the least dishonest, but he worked frankly for his own interest; and it must not be forgotten that in trans-actions with customers who are habitually fuddled and con-fused, a clear-headed man has all the advantage.

Other craftsmen might include a tanner, a shoemaker, and a hatter. Some craftsmen carried their tools with them; a shoeman might set up shop in a family's home and stay until the entire family was properly shod. In some towns, women did not do their own weaving; instead a weaver came periodically and set up a loom in the house. A tailor might come to make up clothes for the man of the house, but most of the clothing, and table and bed linens, were made by the women.

In the early 1800s country towns began to take on an aspect not unlike that of today. Here is Charles Goodrich's description of Ridgefield, Connecticut in *Recollections of a Lifetime:*

Each house was built near the street, with a yard in front and a garden beside it. The fences were low, and of light, open picket slats, made to exclude cattle, pigs, and geese, which then had the freedom of the place. There was a cheerful, confiding, wide, open look all around. Everybody peeped from the win-dows into everybody's grounds. The proprietor was evidently content to be under your eye; nay, as you passed along, his beets and carrots in long beds; his roses and peonies bordering the central walk; the pears and peaches and plums swinging from the trees, all seemed to invite your observation. The barn, having its vast double doors in front, and generally thrown open, presented its interior to your view, with all its gathered treasures of hay, oats, rye, and flax.

Take away the picket fences and animals, turn the gardens and orchards into green lawns with clumps of rhododendron bushes, a magnolia or dogwood tree, tear down the barn or turn it into a garage, cover the windows with curtains and many New England towns of today come into view.

When the English first thought of planting colonies in the New World, one of their fondest dreams was that raw materials from the New World would support industries in the old. Chief among these resources, besides lumber, was wool, which the English hoped to make into fabric to sell back to the colonists.

The New Englanders, however, were inclined to look after them-selves first, relying as little as possible on imports. They started immediately to achieve the talent on how to do the entire cloth-making process.

Once the fleece was sheared in the spring, the preparation of cloth became largely the work of women and girls. First they cleaned it and dyed it. A favorite color was blue, which dye had to be purchased from the store or traveling peddler. A pot of indigo dye, covered, often sat beside the kitchen fireplace; children who didn't want to be punished learned quickly not to tip it over. Other dyes the women created themselves: browns and yellows from hickory and oak wood; violet from iris petals; yellow and orange from sassafras bark; green by combining dye from goldenrod flowers with indigo. The next step after dyeing was to grease and card the wool. A "card" was a rectangular board with short wire teeth which was drawn through the fleece, combing out the tangles and pulling the fibers into parallel rows. One of the early water-powered industries to appear in New England was the carding mill. Girls relieved of this tedious chore could be seen riding by horse to the mill with sacks of fleece billowing up behind them.

Most eighteenth-century homes had two spinning wheels, a small one for flax (linen), which families grew for their own use, and a large walking wheel for wool. Wool was spun standing up. The spinner (spinster) stood next to the wheel, holding a wooden finger in one hand, a loose skein of carded wool in the other. The wool was tied to the top of a spindle. With the finger she tapped the wheel, starting it to spin. Then, taking quick steps backward and forward, she drew the wool across the wheel, which carried it on to a reel. In a single day she might walk as much as twenty miles, and spin six skeins of wool. The yarn was now ready for knitting or weaving.

Females of all ages were involved in the preparation of linen and wool: 4- and 5-year-old girls received their first knitting lessons; older girls and women cleaned and dyed the wool; grandmothers carded it; mothers and aunts spun it. Evenings were spent knitting, sewing linen cloths and bedsheets, and repairing shirts and dresses in front of the fire.

Produce raised by the family was stored in bins in the cellar or hung to dry: potatoes, onions, squash, pumpkins, apples, herbs, beets, beans, and turnips. In addition there were barrels of hard cider, the main beverage besides tea to appear on most tables. The main meals of the day were breakfast, served before daybreak in winter, and dinner, served at noon. A typical supper consisted of bread and butter or bread and milk.

Because there was no refrigeration, New Englanders devised many ways to preserve food. They smoked and salted pork, mutton, beef, and fish. They made applesauce by boiling cider down to a thick syrup and adding slices of apple and quince to cook for just a few minutes. Most animals were slaughtered late in the fall, when they were fat from summer feeding and when the meat could be frozen outdoors.

Food varied tremendously with the seasons. Fall was the time of the best food: fresh fruits and vegetables and fresh meat. In winter fresh foods were eaten as long as possible. By May, meals consisted mostly of dried and salted foods. Strawberries appeared in June, and by midsummer fresh produce began to be available again. Pies and cakes were not part of the daily fare in New England until the nineteenth century, although they were prepared for festivities. Candies and ice cream were unknown, but every child looked forward to sugaring-off time, when he or she could pour a little boiling maple syrup on the snow to make a cold brittle sweet.

To help pay for store purchases, women took tubs of cheese, firkins of butter, and knitted items such as mittens to the store to exchange for credit.

Social gatherings usually centered around work: the raising of a barn, a house, or a meeting house; a quilting bee, usually held in the afternoon; spelling bees and singing schools, conducted at night during the winter; sleigh rides and sledding parties, which might end up with a party at the tavern. Most adult recreation took place in the winter months, for the work of running a farm occupied all members of the family from dawn to dusk in the summer. Children had some time for play all months of the year, yet they had many daily chores as well.

On Sunday there was a service in the morning, followed by dinner; then an afternoon service, followed by supper and evening family prayers. Religious families started and ended each day of the week with family prayer. Everyone retired when the meeting house bell chimed nine o'clock.

School was open two seasons of the year. From May to August young women taught small children to read and count and write. From late fall through early spring male teachers taught children of all ages in one room; those who had farming chores, particularly the older boys, came when they could. School was never open during planting or harvesting season.

Schooling was very limited in the eighteenth century. Many people learned only elementary reading and writing and enough "ciphering" to manage their accounts. Sometimes teachers were scarcely more educated than their students, and there were no standards for teacher training. College education was limited to boys who were planning to become ministers, doctors, lawyers, or merchants. Books were expensive and not widely available. In small towns, the only libraries might be in the homes of the minister and doctor.

The schooling situation improved slightly when university students began opening "select schools" in the summer to earn tuition money and when private academies were established. Students at these schools were exposed to Latin and Greek, learned proper grammar, and sampled modern literature if their teacher and parents were free-minded. Promising students in a small town might also be tutored by the minister. A wealthy family or the town might provide money to send a student who couldn't afford tuition to Harvard, Yale, Dartmouth, Brown, or Bowdoin. Higher education for women didn't begin until 1837 with the opening of Mount Holyoke Female Seminary in South Hadley, Massachusetts.

Beginning with the Puritans most business of the town was taken up at the annual town meeting, which everyone was invited to attend. Selectmen were chosen to manage town affairs for the next year along with a school committee, road surveyors, and a clerk. In the 1800s and early 1900s the primary business included school and road maintenance and the care of the poor. Welfare was a major responsibility of the town, often involving care for up to thirty percent of the population, including the elderly. At the town meeting, impoverished persons were auctioned off. Whoever placed the lowest bid for an individual became responsible for feeding and clothing that person for the year, and received some money from the town for doing so. Because the care of indigents was considered the responsibility of the entire community, not the family, the person won at auction might be a parent.

After religious and civil affairs began to be separated, the town meeting had its religious counterpart in the parish meeting. Here maintenance of the church, including fixing the minister's salary, was decided. Although the congregation did have the power to remove a preacher from the pulpit if he proved unsatisfactory, the power wasn't used very often. There is a story, however, about a parish that found a minister too liberal and removed him. When they found a replacement, one woman who was usually outspoken kept silent while the others extolled the virtues of the new man. Finally someone asked if she didn't support him and she said, "I'll wait until he needs support." Several months later the congregation began to talk about replacing the new minister. The woman who had kept quiet before spoke up. She said, "You remind me of the young man who got married and was so in love with his wife he wanted to eat her up. A few months later he wished he had."

Life in rural New England towns today bears little resemblance to life in earlier eras, despite the many physical features that are unchanged and the town meetings that are still held. One town that actually recreates life in a New England farming community around the 1820s is Old Sturbridge Village in Massachusetts. Visitors can view and participate in village activities.

DOWN TO THE SEA IN SHIPS
New Englanders have always clung to the coast. In early days, the ocean afforded a natural defense against Indians and wild animals. And the ships were a lifeline to England, bringing clothing and tools and letters from home. The waters off New England were so filled with fish that Thomas Morton, writing in 1636, said, "I myself at the turning of the tide have seen such multitudes of sea bass that it seemed to me that one might go over their backs dry-shod." Fishing was encouraged in early colonial days by exempting fishermen from military service and not taxing vessels and stock for seven years. The chief catch was cod, which was salted and dried and sold in Catholic countries for days of fast and abstinence.

Shipbuilding quickly became a major business in New England. One of the Plymouth settlers' initial desire was that a ship's carpenter be brought from England to live with them. By the middle of the eighteenth century New England was launching seventy new ships a year. Ships built in Rhode Island, Massachusetts, and Maine carried produce back and forth among all thirteen colonies along the Atlantic seaboard. They also transported lumber, tobacco, rice, tar, pitch, and other resources from the American colonies to the world's markets. England encouraged the development of the carrier trade, but restricted the sale of some commodities. For the most part these restrictions did not hamper New England trade. Merchants and sea captains often ignored the restrictions, and traded with anyone who would buy.

After the Revolution, New England shipping enjoyed an era of unprecedented prosperity. Chief among the new markets was China, where fur to line silk robes was much in demand as well as sails, ropes, anchors, and a multitude of European wares. Some merchants travelled to Canton by way of Europe, trading at ports along the way, arriving with a cargo that brought high prices. Others circled the tip of South America, sailed to the northwest coast of North America, purchased furs from Indians, and sailed to China. Some ships rarely saw their home ports. But the profits from their travels returned to line the pockets and furnish the brick mansions of merchants in Newport, Salem, Boston, Hartford, and Providence. Among the treasures from the Orient that ended up in New England were works of art. Today, Boston's Museum of Fine Arts has one of the finest collections of Chinese art in the world.

When whaling first began in the seventeenth century, whales could be captured close to the New England coast. The whale population grew scarce in these waters, but the demand for whale oil for candles and lamps increased. Whalers from Nantucket and New Bedford, Massachusetts; Bristol, Rhode Island, and Stonington, Connecticut pursued the large mammals to the waters off Brazil and eventually around the Cape and into the Pacific. By the time Herman Melville set off on the whaler

Acushnet in 1841, a boy of fourteen signing on for his first voyage could expect to be a young man of seventeen before he saw his family again. Whaling continued to be a major New England industry until the appearance of kerosene in the 1850s, and continued on a smaller scale until the last voyage of the *Charles W. Morgan* in the 1920s. Today, whaling museums exist in New Bedford and Nantucket.

In the mid-nineteenth century, New England shipbuilders began producing the graceful three-masted, square-rigged Yankee clipper ships, the fastest in the history of the world. When the gold rush began in California the clippers were used for fast delivery of cargo around Cape Horn to San Francisco. In 1851, the *Flying Cloud,* built by Donald McKay in East Boston, sailed from New York to San Francisco in 89 days, breaking all records. The era of clipper ships began to fade with the advent of the steamship and the transcontinental railroad. Mystic, Connecticut is today a seaport museum recalling clipper ship days.

Home life in coastal towns followed many of the same patterns found in farming communities, with significant differences. The absence of men in some households for two or three years at a time taught women to be skilled at all phases of raising and providing for a family. The small industries in coastal towns revolved around shipping more than farming, with such businesses as ropewalks, sail lofts, rigging shops, and cooper shops. The atmosphere of a coastal town, where ships bearing exotic cargo were anchored in the harbor, and sea captains told children stories of South Sea islands and European ports, differed from the insular world of a farming village. And whereas farming towns tended to be spread out, coastal towns were crowded, with narrow winding streets and houses tucked close together. Marblehead, Massachusetts; Nantucket Island; and Newport, Rhode Island all retain the character of old seaport towns.

By the end of the eighteenth century economic differences between the two worlds were beginning to be felt. In farming communities, a good part of the family's business could be conducted by exchange; money was relatively unimportant. There were no great differences in wealth. One or two families might be prosperous, but most people worked their own land and lived in a style nearly identical to that of their neighbors. In coastal trading centers, money accrued to a few merchants and shipowners who became spectacularly wealthy. Most profit was poured into new trading ventures, but there were great differences to be seen in the way people lived and dressed.

Another major difference was the type of skills people were learning. Engaging in international trade required managerial talent, understanding of complicated and varied transactions, familiarity with currencies, languages, and customs from all parts of the world, and a willingness to take huge financial risks in the quest for even greater profits. Trades people and artisans found more work around coastal towns, producing handcrafted goods for export, and developing a much greater range of products. Opportunities for education were greater for more people, partly because there were more wealthy families. Also, coastal towns could afford more educational resources and people were in contact with the outside world. Altogether, the demands and opportunities in coastal towns, particularly in trading centers, were contributing to the development of a new breed of American: the New England capitalist.

WATER POWER

The Anglo-Saxon race has accepted the primal curse as a blessing, has deified work, and would not have thanked Adam for abstaining from the apple.

JAMES RUSSELL LOWELL (1819-1891)

Rhode Island was the first state to reach a crossroads in its development. Living primarily from the sea, Rhode Island merchants amassed tremendous fortunes in the eighteenth century and a reputation for being cutthroat adventurers. They were skilled at juggling markets, at establishing an international network of agents, at turning every transaction into a profit. They enjoyed the risks of profiteering and smuggling.

Most of the state's population was involved in the mercantile business either directly or by supplying services and goods. The leading centers of commercial activity in the colonial era were Newport and Providence. During the Revolution, Newport was destroyed by the British, a blow from which it never fully recovered. One reason was that it was located on an island.

Providence could develop connections to inland towns where more and more products were being manufactured. Transportation improved rapidly with the building of turnpikes and bridges. But Newport was isolated from these resources. And when it became clear that England and the United States were going to war again in 1812, many people moved their businesses out of Newport, fearing another siege.

Providence mercantile firms continued to dispatch agents to the Caribbean, South America, Europe, and China. But trade became increasingly difficult. At the turn of the nineteenth century Europe was embroiled in the Napoleonic wars; trade with any of the countries involved was a highly dangerous undertaking. In 1808, the U.S. Congress declared an embargo on foreign trade that nearly killed New England shipping altogether. Market conditions during these years were completely unstable, adding another element of risk. Other ports, particularly New York, were providing keener competition than Providence had experienced in the past. And world trade was beginning to be regulated, a trend that ran counter to Rhode Island's entreprenurial instincts.

Merchants began withdrawing from international shipping and looking for other ways to invest their capital. One of the earliest and shrewdest merchants to change direction was Moses Brown. England had cornered the world's textile market since the development of factories where spinning and weaving were done on water-powered machines. New England handmade fabrics couldn't compete. Not only was production slower, quality could not be controlled. Homespun materials were rough; machines were turning out beautiful, smooth materials that could be printed. Brown thought Rhode Island was ideally suited to the development of a textile industry to rival Manchester, England. The state had a wealth of water power, the humid climate kept yarns supple, and there were skilled spinners and weavers in the state who were already involved in a cottage textile industry: carding and dyeing were done at a mill, but spinning and weaving were done in people's homes.

Brown had the good fortune to hire a young Englishman named Samuel Slater. Slater had worked for years in cotton factories in Derbyshire and knew all aspects of the manufacturing end of the business thoroughly. England would not allow plans of its machines to leave the country, but Slater had memorized the Arkwright spinning machine. With the help of a blacksmith named Oziel Wilkinson, Slater built a new mill in Pawtucket, Rhode Island, for spinning cotton yarn. Rhode Island was on its way to becoming a center of textile manufacturing.

The invention of the cotton gin in 1794 was another critical step in the development of this industry. Southern plantations were now producing enough cotton to supply the burgeoning mills: The same invention that prolonged the existence of slavery stimulated the growth of the textile industry.

Francis Cabot Lowell, a Boston merchant, also went to England and memorized the plans for both the Arkwright spinning machine and the power loom. In 1814, the first textile company to perform the entire process of transforming cotton fiber into finished cloth was opened in Waltham, Massachusetts. Three years later Lowell died, but his partners, Patrick Jackson and Nathan Appleton, who had built fortunes on trade, began planning a new factory complex on the Merrimack River. Around the mills they built an entire town and named it after Lowell.

This first company town to appear in New England represented a concerted effort to build a community that would be pleasant to live in. Lowell and his partners refused to employ children or to recruit cheap labor from Europe. Instead they drew on young women from the farming communities. The workers lived in company dormitories, shopped in company stores, attended company churches, and took courses in the evenings. Many stayed only for a few years, to earn money to send a brother to college and to help pay debts on their family's farm. Eventually competition from other factories grew so intense that Lowell began to turn into a crowded, immigrant-filled town. Its Boston backers never had the same paternalistic feeling toward Irish and French-Canadian workers, and the humanitarian spirit went out of Lowell.

Near Lowell is the town of Lawrence, which was created out of land taken from two neighboring towns, Andover and Methuen. Under the direction of former army engineer Charles Bigelow, the longest dam on the Merrimack was built. Like Lowell, Lawrence was built with Boston money and designed as a model town. Housing areas and industrial areas were kept separate. The investors petitioned the state to set up public schools and provide "suitable accommodations for the reception and relief of the poor and sick and those disabled by accidents or sudden illness." They attracted doctors to the town and established a police force. But eventually Lawrence changed to an immigrant town and Bostonians lost interest in its problems.

The Amoskeag mills, built further north on the Merrimack, grew to become the biggest cotton-textile manufacturing company in the world. When the first mill was built, before power looms had been installed, the residents of the small town of Derryfield voted at a town meeting to change the name to Manchester, predicting that the town would come to rival the English textile center. All trace of the eighteenth-century town disappeared as one red brick mill after another was built and Manchester developed into New Hampshire's largest city.

Textile manufacturing was not the only industry to develop. In Connecticut, a tremendous variety of businesses grew up. Firearms, clocks and watches, tinware, brass, silverware, and vulcanized rubber are just a few of the products that poured out in the 1800s. By end of the century Connecticut claimed more patents in proportion to its population than any other state.

Mass-produced shoes became another leading business for New Englanders. Banking and insurance were becoming big business, centered in Hartford and Boston. Alexander Graham Bell invented the telephone, Samuel F. B. Morse the telegraph.

As a center for industry, New England's social character began to change. From a homogeneous region of small towns, whose families were largely self-supporting, New England grew into a complex of cities that attracted immigrants from Ireland, Germany, Russia, Poland, Italy, French Canada, and Portugal. After the Civil War black Americans came to New England to find work in its cities. All of these groups of people faced tremendous problems. They were underpaid, socially ostracized, harassed, and exploited. There were exceptions; some towns and individuals were more welcoming than others. But the first generation's experience in New England was generally a painful one. And those who experienced discrimination exercised it against those who came later. Some people left New England as quickly as they arrived, heading for the more open and, they hoped, more tolerant west. But most of them stayed, making a substantial contribution to New England's industrial growth and changing it into a multi-ethnic society enriched by the heritage of many cultures.

Religion continued to be an active force in community life but diversified to embrace all major faiths and denominations. By the 1970s Massachusetts, once the stronghold of Puritanism, would become sixty-five percent Catholic.

At the same time that immigrants and black Americans were pouring into the mushrooming industrial areas, farmers were packing their families into wagons and heading west. Living off the land had never been a profit-making business; farmers had depended on selling some of their produce as well as their handcrafted gadgets, tools, and fabrics. Factories destroyed the market for handicrafts. The opening of the fertile farmlands of the west began to cut into the sale of produce and meat, particularly after railroads began crossing the country. Vermont, whose population had boomed in the late 1700s, lost population steadily during the 1800s and never developed enough industry to attract new residents. Some towns disappeared altogether. The fields that had been created with so much pain and care became overgrown with weeds and brush. Cellars became grassy pits. Gradually the woods reclaimed the land. Other towns maintained a small but steady population who turned increasingly to dairy and truck farming and to the cultivation of orchards. Today, working farms are increasingly rare. Land commands high prices. Farmers sell out and retire to a warm climate, while their pastures are converted into building lots for vacation home communities.

NEW ENGLAND TODAY

Since the 1940s both textile manufacturing and shoe manufacturing have declined sharply. The cities that grew up around the factories now suffer high unemployment rates. There is talk of turning Lowell into an urban national park. But the Amoskeag mills of Manchester, perhaps the most beautiful example of mill architecture, face imminent destruction.

In Connecticut and Massachusetts, small towns near urban

centers have become beautiful commuter towns for middle-class families who like the small town atmosphere and are glad to escape the congestion and problems of city living. In the cities, redevelopment plans have been hotly contested political issues since the early 1960s. Some old and decaying neighborhoods have been torn down and replaced with mammoth structures of reinforced concrete or steel and glass. Others have been restored by energetic families who like the excitement and diversity of cities and don't want their neighborhoods destroyed. Some new industries involved in electronics, space exploration, and defense grew up in these two states, bringing prosperity and industrial parks. But business in these areas has also dropped off. Land in the Connecticut Valley that was being farmed ten years ago is turning into housing developments.

In Rhode Island, an issue of great concern is whether or not the Narragansett Electric Company should be allowed to build a nuclear power plant near Ninigret Pond in Charlestown. Among the questions being asked are: What are the short- and long-term hazards to the population? What means of protection are being planned? For example, how will waste be disposed? What impact will construction and use have on the land? Ecologists fear that the natural balance of life in the salt water pond will be destroyed forever while plant proponents say it can be restored in a few years. The governor's position is that no one yet knows enough about the social and environmental consequences of building a nuclear power plant to make a decision for or against it. Extensive studies are underway, both by the electric company and by the Coastal Resource Center of the University of Rhode Island.

In Maine, coastal towns have small, year-round populations who live from fishing, farming, and small businesses. The summer tourist trade is an increasingly major part of the state's economy. There is both a felt need to attract development and a concern about preserving the state's natural resources. Residents of Searsport recently voted against having an oil refinery built off their coast. As one teenager said, "My brother left Maine to live in New York and he really likes it. But when he's sick of the city he comes back to Maine because it isn't New York. Who's going to come here if it starts to look like New York?" There is a growing interest in farming and fishing. Students in Kennebunkport, Maine, have begun publishing a magazine containing interviews with residents who live by lobstering, deep sea fishing, and truck farming.

Southern New Hampshire has long been a playground for city workers; but residents are beginning to worry about the toll recreation takes on their state. The most recent issue is whether or not to continue Interstate Highway 93 through Franconia Notch in the White Mountains, one of the most popular, most beautiful regions of New England, and part of a national forest. The principle reason for public concern is that overlooking the notch is a granite face formed by a series of ridges. Worshipped by Indians, immortalized by Nathaniel Hawthorne in "The Great Stone Face," the Old Man of the Mountain draws thousands of visitors each year. Residents fear that highway construction and pollution from increased traffic will damage the face. New Hampshire has also made a recent decision about the development of an oil refinery. When the state gave permission to Aristotle Onassis to build a refinery off the coast of Portsmouth, Portsmouth residents argued that the state had no legal right to grant authorization without their consent. They won their case.

In Vermont tourism, winter sports, and vacation homes are now the leading source of revenue. Some residents feel development has gone too far; others feel the state should continue to encourage it, but with regulations to safeguard both the environment and the people who will be using the new facilities.

Throughout New England there is growing concern about the future, about finding ways to protect the environment, to preserve the landmarks of its rich past, and to deal with the problems and needs of modern living. Some people are leaving the cities, looking for a life that is less fragmented, less dependent on some other person's labor, and more attuned to the rhythm of nature than the hum of machines. Others, in New England tradition, are concerned with progress and development, with producing goods and supplying services, with continuing to be world leaders in many fields. And many others are simply struggling to "make it," finding it a full-time job. New England today is searching for its future, finding more questions than certainties.

Clam digging at Lubec, near
the border between Maine
and the province of New
Brunswick. Left: Slopes of
Mt. Katahdin (5,268 feet)
highest point in Maine.

Grand Falls on the Dead
River, between Flagstaff
Lake and The Forks, Maine.
This area of the river is
inaccessible except by
canoe. Right: Moose.
feeding along Allagash
River, Maine.

Canada Geese at Dead Creek Wildlife Refuge in Addison, Vermont.

Seagulls soar and dive as they follow commercial fishing boat near Cape Cod, Massachusetts. Left: Sand dunes synonymous with the Cape, famous as a summer vacation area.

"The Corner House" a historical landmark in Stockbridge, Massachusetts. Right: Relics of past dominate window of coffee house in Stockbridge.

Reconstructed facsimile of
the Old North Bridge at
Concord, Massachusetts,
spans the Concord River.
Left: Replica of Mayflower
at Plymouth, Massachusetts.
On December 21, 1620
Pilgrims landed here to
establish the first permanent
settlement in New England.

Abandoned farm, near
Underhill, Vermont. Right:
Walden Pond, near Concord,
Massachusetts. Henry Thoreau
lived some months in a hut
nearby while he enjoyed a
hermits life.

Minutemen statue at Concord, Massachusetts, commemorates the death of the first English soldier. This act triggered the Revolutionary war and is known as "The shot heard around the world." Left: Duplicate of original Plymouth Plantation village in Massachusetts.

Sun pierces passing storm clouds on farm near Shelburne, Vermont. Right: Anglers on the Housatonic River near West Cornwall, Connecticut.

52

Spring pastoral scene in
Vermont. Right: Alpine
Azalea in the White Moun-
tains, New Hampshire.
These tiny blossoms are no
larger than a kitchen match
head. One must often be on
hands and knees
to find them.

Grove of young maples in the Berkshires.

Bee at work in dandelion blossom. Left: Spring apple blossoms at West Barnet, Vermont. Pages 60-61: Chelsea, Vermont, nestled in foothills of the Green Mountains.

Diapensia adapts to the alpine slopes above timberline on Presidential Range, New Hampshire. Blossoms match the diameter of pennies and dimes. Right: Morning mist envelopes rail fence near Flagstaff, Maine.

Lobster fisherman pulling traps off Point Judith, Rhode Island. Right: Recent catch of lobster and crabs on dock at Point Judith, Rhode Island.

Early winter snow carpets Newport, Rhode Island. In background one of the magnificent mansions along the famous "Cliff Walk". Left: Snow covered rocks along the ocean shore at Newport.

Windmill appears to dominate the Prescott farm, Middletown, Rhode Island. Right: This well preserved house on Block Island, Rhode Island, is typical of many in the area.

Church of Christ and town hall in Mt. Washington, Massachusetts. Left: Horses adapt to snow-covered pasture on farm near Bennington, Vermont. In distance, Bennington Battle Monument 360 feet high on site of storehouse successfully defended by America during Revolutionary War. Pages 72-23: Fearless kayaker on the West River, Jamaica, Vermont.

Looking west from Mt. Mansfield, across Champlain Valley. Lake Champlain in the distance lies between the New York, Vermont borders. Right: Midday sun delivers aura of brilliance to fall foliage along shore of Silver Lake, near Middlebury, Vermont.

Sun rises over the Green
Mountains casting morning
light on Lake Champlain's
Shelburne Bay, Vermont.
Left: Ketch, "Gemarama"
on Lake Champlain, near
Burlington, Vermont.

Mountain stream cascading down slopes of White Mountains. Right: Old Man of the Mountain, state symbol of New Hampshire, natural rock formation in Franconia Notch on Cannon Mountain.

Delicate blooming gold
thread in the White
Mountains, New Hamp-
shire. Left: Morning dew on
blade of grass. Cohesive
drop at tip defies gravity.

Sunset reflections on ice encrusted weed. Right: Late afternoon sun glistens on snow covered slopes of the Franconia Range in New Hampshire.

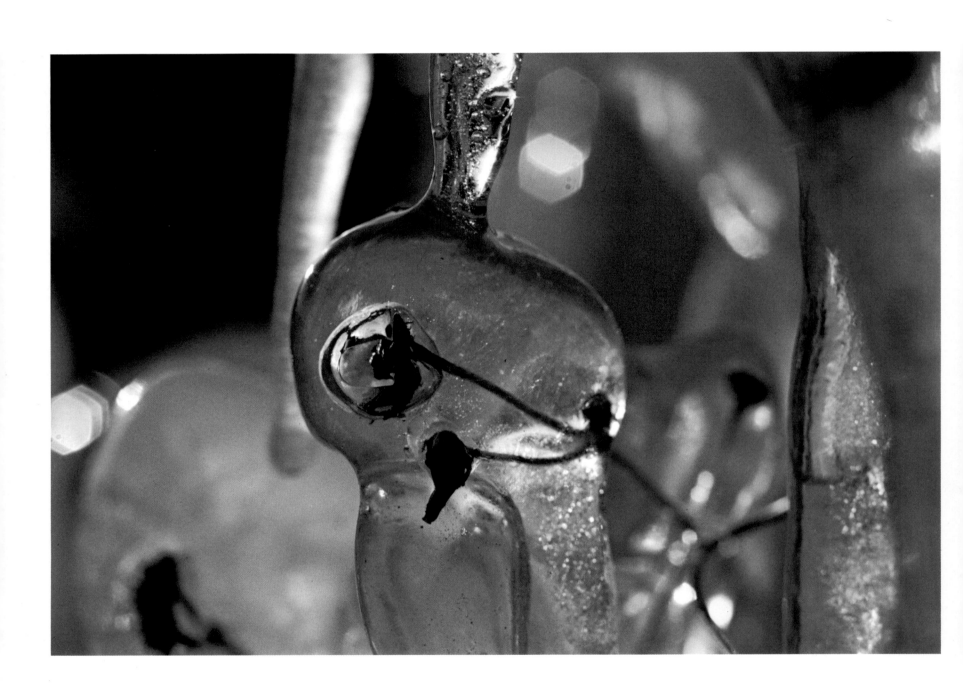

Mountaineers on summit ridge of Mt. Mansfield. Left: Sunlit Mt. Mansfield, (4,393 feet), highest peak in Vermont's Green Mountain Range. Pages 88-89: Climbers pass wind sculptured snow on Mt. Washington (6,288 feet), highest peak in New Hampshire.

A new fallen maple leaf cradled by a hemlock bough. Right: Chimney Pond, at the base of Mt. Katahdin's eastern cirque.

Fall foliage along the Kancamagus Highway between Lincoln and Conway, New Hampshire. Left: Daring white water canoeists running log dam on Androscoggin River, New Hampshire.

Abandoned house appears determined to maintain its right of survival on Block Island, Rhode Island. Right: Early morning vapor drifts through conifers in Maine wilderness.

St. John River, Maine.
Left: Courage fosters
spectacular dive into old
swimming hole on Rock River
near Newfane, Vermont.

White-tail deer swimming across Lake Chamberlain, part of Allegash waterway in Maine. Right: Sunrise along Allagash River, prior to entering the St. John, near Allagash Village, Maine.

West peak of Bigelow Range (4,150 feet), near Stratton, Maine. Right: Low tide reveals seaweed along the shore of Bailey Island, Maine.

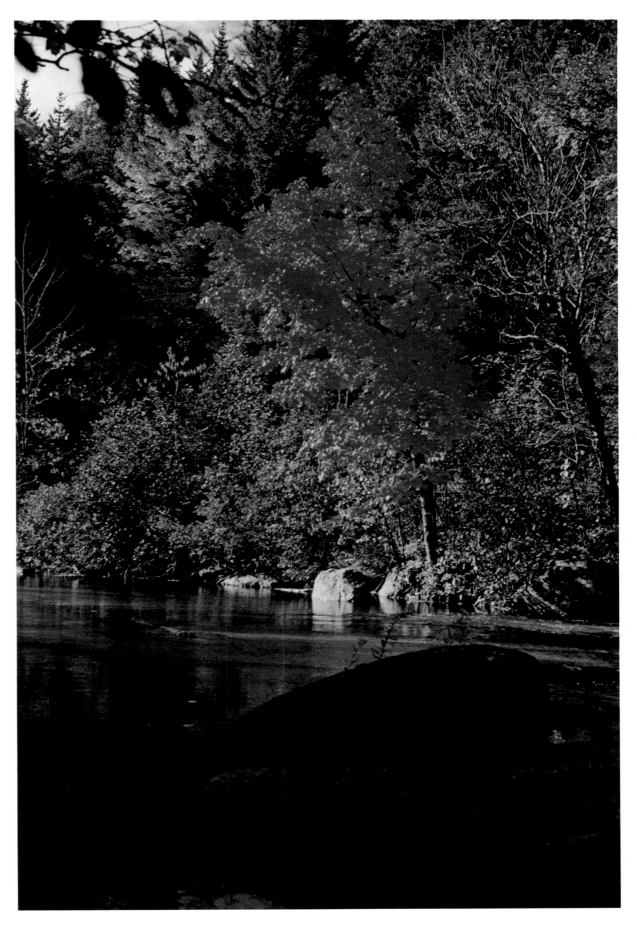

Brilliant maple along the Swift River in the Pemigewasset Wilderness, New Hampshire. Left: Autumn tinted sugar maple on farm, near Newark, Vermont.

Autumn splendor on back road near Waitsfield, Vermont.

Bash Bish Falls in the Western Berkshires, near Mt. Everett, Massachusetts. Right: Autumn foliage provides splashes of color in the Southern Berkshires.

Spring-fed stream in the Southern Berkshires, Massachusetts. Left: Highrise development delivers commanding view of Charles River in Cambridge, Massachusetts.

Old Stone Mill or Mystery Tower, in Newport, Rhode Island. It is believed to be oldest standing structure in the United States; possibly old Norse church built around 1050 A.D. Right: Sunset display above farm on Connecticut Island near Jamestown, Rhode Island.

Reconstructed Revolutionary War frigate "Rose" at King's Dock, Newport, Rhode Island. Left, Evening sun highlights fishing fleet moored at Point Judith, Rhode Island.

Autumn foliage lends brilliance to South Royalton, Vermont. Right: Dense mist veils early morning sun.

Early winter on summit ridge of Franconia Range in New Hampshire. Left: Climbers scale slopes of White Mountains in New Hampshire.

Sunlight casts an ominous
glow over farm near
Rutland, Vermont. Right:
Cross-country ski tracks
near Shelburne, Vermont.

Snow encrusted conifers near summit of Green Mountains in Vermont.

Lights aglow deliver
delightful contrast in home
at Lower Waterford Village,
Vermont. Left: Sunlit woods
in early morning, carpeted
with fresh snowfall. Pages
124-125: Snowcapped
stones appear to be floating
in the gentle current.

Midwinter contrasts in
Burke Hollow, Vermont.
Right: Winter comes to
Newark Village, Vermont.

Sunrise highlights early frost on grove of poplar trees near Middlebury, Vermont. Left: Morning sun bursts over Camel's Hump (4,083 feet), Vermont's fourth highest mountain peak.

Frost crystals. Right:
Coming down the wild
Black Branch River in early
winter, near Island Pond,
Vermont.

Mountaineer atop frosty chimney in foothills of Franconia Range, New Hampshire. Left: Cross-country skiers leave bridge spanning Pemigewasset River in Franconia Notch, New Hampshire.

Sunrise and mist through pines in winter thaw. Right: Winter sunset on snow covered Mt. Mansfield viewed from floor of Pleasant Valley.

Franconia, New Hampsire, Mount Lafayette (5,249 feet).

Autumn foliage teeming
with beauty in Waits River
Village, Vermont. Left: Farm
near Bristol, Vermont.

Solitude along country road in early morning near Shelburne, Vermont. Right: Sunset and approaching storm near St. Johnsbury, Vermont.

Rainbow trout leaps a
waterfall on Willoughby
River, in Orleans, Vermont.
Right: Golden Mountain
Ash in autumn splendor
bordering Appalachian
Mountain Trail in Maine.

Sugar maple with early
autumn foliage. Right:
Cantilever Rock on the face
of Mt. Mansfield, Vermont.

Afterglow from sunset over
Mooselookmeguntic Lake,
near Rangely, Maine. Left:
Water released from dam on
Flagstaff Lake heralds a
thunderous beginning of the
Dead River, Maine.

Indian paintbrush and daisies along shore of saltwater bay near Eastport, Maine. Right: Thistle tenders delicate contrast against evening sky.

Reflection on mirror-like pond near Franconia, New Hampshire. Left: Morning fog rises from frigid Ammonoosuc River, Bretton Woods, New Hampshire.

Peaks of Presidential Range, looking east from Danville, Vermont.

Stark patterns etched
against the evening sky.
Right: Tamarack (sometimes
called larch), Franconia,
New Hampshire. Pages
156-157: Skiers on slopes
of Mt. Snow, Vermont.

154

Defoliated sugar maples await the coming of spring during heavy snowfall. Left: Snowcapped stones on the West River near Jamaca, Vermont.

Spring growth along mountain stream in White Mountains of New Hampshire. Left: Orioles constructing a nest in a blossoming sugar maple.

Farm near Monroe, New
Hampshire, along shore of
the Connecticut River.
Right: Dense foliage
parallels abandoned
railroad right of way at
Stockbridge, Massachusetts.

Winter sunrise streaks across pond near Pelham, New Hampshire. Left: Diapensia, an alpine flower, on the Presidential Range, New Hampshire.

Evening shadows lie across a blanket of snow.

Long hilly ridges wooded to the summit, with deep valleys, mark the Berkshires in Massachusetts. Right: Fishing boat heading home at sunset, Narragansett Bay, Rhode Island. Pages 172-173: "Snow Rollers" or hollowed snowballs, near Stowe, Vermont. This rare formation originates from fresh snow at the precise temperature, plus gale winds, which blow them across open fields. Some have measured well-nigh four feet in diameter.

Riding the crest of breakers offers a challenge for surfers at Newport, Rhode Island. Left: Palatial estates border Atlantic shore at Newport, Rhode Island.

Farm near Jamestown, Rhode Island. In foreground, tidewater of Narragansett Bay. Right: Raging floodwaters of Winooski River seem to explode as they pass Essex Junction, Vermont.

Sailing vessels "Hesper"
and "Luther Little" in
repose at Wiscasset, Maine.
Left: Ground fog hovers
over back road near
Shelburne, Vermont.

Atlantic breaker meets an offshore obstruction on the coast of Maine. Right: Owls Head Light guides mariners to safety of Penobscot Bay, Maine.

Midwinter morning on farm near South Hope, Maine. Left: Lobster traps awaiting departure of lobstermen, to garner this world famous delicacy.

A calm tidal basin near Rockland, Maine.

Midwinter morning on farm near South Hope, Maine. Left: Lobster traps awaiting departure of lobstermen, to garner this world famous delicacy.

A calm tidal basin near Rockland, Maine.

Silent sentinel atop Cape Elizabeth, near Portland, Maine. Right: Colorful buoys mark the home of a lobster fisherman. Pages 188-189: Cape Neddick Light, commonly known as the "Nubble", erected in 1879 near York, Maine.

Light dusting of snow on Minuteman statue in Concord, Massachusetts. Left: Old North Church, Boston, erected in 1723; in this belfry the lanterns were hung, "One if by land and two if by sea", to warn of the approach of the British and start Paul Revere on his famous ride.

Late evening fog envelops
Scarboro, Maine.

PHOTOGRAPHIC DATA

All illustrations in this presentation were projected from
35 mm transparencies photographed without the aid of any
filters. Film was Kodak Kodachrome II, ASA speed 25.
Unusual and dramatic photographs are identified by page
numbers with the following additional information.

Page 10, Nikon F, 135mm lens, 1/500 sec.

Page 14, Nikon F, 50mm lens, 1/1000 sec.

Page 15, Nikon F, 20mm lens, 1/1000 sec.

Page 38, Nikon F, 135mm lens, 1/500 sec.

Pages 40-41, Nikon F, 50mm lens, 1/500 sec.

Page 43, Nikon F, 50mm lens, 1/500 sec.

Pages 72-73, Honeywell Pentax, 200mm lens, 1/500 sec.

Page 74, Nikkormat, 135mm lens, 1/500 sec.

Page 76, Honeywell Pentax, 135mm lens, 1/500 sec.

Pages 88-89, Honeywell Pentax, 50mm lens, 30° below zero.

Page 92, Honeywell Pentax, 135mm lens, 1/500 sec.

Page 96, Honeywell Pentax, 50mm lens, 1/500 sec.

Page 116, Nikon F, 50mm lens, 1/500 sec.

Page 118, Nikkormat, 50mm lens, 1/500 sec. 10° below zero
in 40 m.p.h. wind.

Page 126, Nikon F, 20mm lens, 1/500 sec.

Page 131, Honeywell Pentax, 50mm lens, 1/500 sec.

Page 142, Nikon F, 50mm lens, 1/1000 sec.

Page 146, Honeywell Pentax, 50mm lens, 1/500 sec.

Pages 156-157, Nikon F, 135mm lens, 1/500 sec.

Page 175, Nikon F, 200mm lens, 1/500 sec.

Page 177, Nikon F, 135mm lens, 1/500 sec.

Page 180, Nikon F, 135mm lens, 1/500 sec.